The Odd

BUTT NAKED!

FWOOMF!

by allan plenderleith

ℛℛ
RAVETTE PUBLISHING

**THE ODD SQUAD and all related characters ©2001
by Allan Plenderleith   www.theoddsquad.co.uk**

First Published by
Ravette Publishing Limited 2003
Unit 3, Tristar Centre, Star Road, Partridge Green, West Sussex RH13 8RA

Printed in Malta

ISBN: 1 84161 190 5

MAUDE INVENTS A
GET-RICH-QUICK SCHEME FOR
LONG HAUL FLIGHTS

DUG'S MUM WALKS INTO HIS ROOM WHILE HE WAS 'CHOKING THE CHICKEN'

UNFORTUNATELY, IN THE CONFUSION AND TERROR OF BEING CHASED BY A DOG, GINGER HAD MISTAKEN THE AIR VENT FOR THE CAT FLAP

ALTHOUGH DISTRESSING AT THE TIME, LATER EVERYONE WOULD AGREE THAT THE DOG FARTING ITSELF INTO THE FIRE WAS ACTUALLY BLOODY HILARIOUS

The DO's and DON'T's
OF LOVE MAKING!

USE LUBRICATION
AND BABY OIL!

USE TOO MUCH!

TRY SEX
EQUIPMENT!

LOSE THE
INSTRUCTIONS!

DO

HAVE SEX
IN THE CAR!

DON'T

LEAN ON
THE HANDBRAKE!

DO

HAVE SEX IN
A PUBLIC
TOILET!

DON'T

HAVE A POO
WHILE YOU'RE
THERE!

BILLY WONDERED IF HE'D FOLLOWED THROUGH ON THAT LAST FART

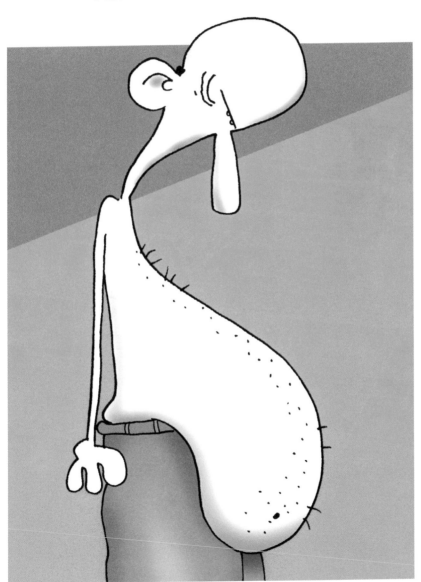

AFTER LIMPING FOR SEVERAL BLOCKS, MAUDE WAS RELIEVED TO FIND HER HIGH HEEL WASN'T BROKEN AFTER ALL

HOW TO TELL WHEN YOU'RE
DRUNK!

1. YOU WONDER WHY EVERYONE LOOKS LIKE A GIANT, THEN REALISE YOU'RE ON THE FLOOR!

2. YOUR SNOGGING TECHNIQUE BECOMES SOMEWHAT ENTHUSIASTIC!

3. SUDDENLY EVERYONE IS YOUR FRIEND!

4. YOU FEEL THE NEED TO EXPOSE YOUR NAKED BITS TO MEMBERS OF THE PUBLIC!

5. KEBABS SEEM LIKE A MOUTH-WATERING DELICACY!

DUG DISCOVERS THAT SEX DOLLS THESE DAYS ARE INCREDIBLY REALISTIC

UNFORTUNATELY, MAUDE'S SKIRT WAS SO SHORT THAT WHEN SHE BENT DOWN EVERYONE SAW HER KEBAB

DUG'S GIRLFRIEND WAS REALLY WILD IN BED

LILY COULD TELL BILLY HAD BEEN
WATCHING A SCARY MOVIE IN
HIS BEDROOM AGAIN

The MANY FACES of MEN during SEX!

OH YEAH.
KEEP DOING
THAT FOREVER.

YEAH! YOU
LIKE THAT!
DO YOU!
DO YOU!

OW! STOP
HOLDING ONTO
MY BUM HAIRS!

OH, DO I HAVE
TO GO DOWN
THERE?

OH NO, THE CONDOM'S JUST SLIPPED OFF!

DON'T PULL IT BACK SO FAR!

WHAT DO YOU MEAN 'HURRY UP, EASTENDERS IS ON'?!!

GET OFF! STUPID DOG!

YES! YES! YES!

WELL, THAT'S ME DONE. GOODNIGHT!

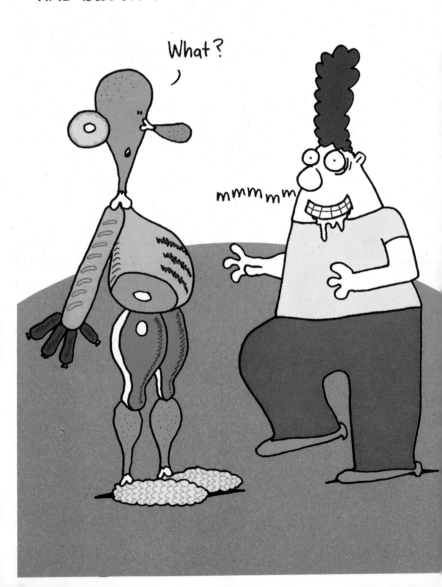

THE ODD SQUAD GUIDE TO MEN IN BED

★ Mr. QUICKIE ★

HE MAKES LOVE IN LIGHTNING FAST TIME.
BLINK AND YOU MAY MISS IT.

★ CAPTAIN KINKY ★

KNOWS EVERY POSITION IN THE BOOK
AND A FEW THAT AREN'T! HAS AN ARSENAL
OF EQUIPMENT THAT MAY CAUSE INJURY

★ KING of the OUTDOORS ★
PREFERS TO DO IT IN UNUSUAL PLACES WITH A HIGH CHANCE OF BEING CAUGHT.

★ The DRUNKEN FUMBLER ★
AFTER FIFTEEN PINTS HE CAN STILL PERFORM – WELL, ALMOST. LIKES TO FART AND GIGGLE THROUGHOUT.

BILLY WAS DELIGHTED TO
FIND A NEW TOY
IN HIS MUM'S BEDROOM

MAUDE WAS JUST ABOUT
TO SAY HOW NICE THE NEW
HOT TUB WAS, WHEN SHE
NOTICED SOMETHING

AT THE BARBER'S JEFF ASKED FOR A "NUMBER TWO"

MAUDE DIDN'T NEED TASSELS ON HER NIPPLES TO PERFORM HER DRUNKEN STRIPTEASE – THANKS TO HER EXCESS NIPPLE HAIR!

WHEN HAVING SEX IN THE
BATH BE CAREFUL NOT TO
THRUST TOO HARD

JEFF WAKES UP WITH A BIG STIFFIE

SNOW IN THE SUMMER?
HOW STRANGE, THOUGHT LILY

IF YOU'RE GOING TO PLAY
FOOTSIE UNDER THE TABLE,
REMEMBER TO TRIM YOUR
TOENAILS FIRST

HOW TO MAKE YOUR OWN

Porn Movie!

Costumes

MEN, WEAR THE FOLLOWING:
- HANDLEBAR MOUSTACHE
- BOILER SUIT
- CHEESY GRIN

WOMEN: WEAR AS LITTLE
AS POSSIBLE, PREFERABLY
RED AND SEE-THROUGH
(IE. STUFF YOU NORMALLY
WOULDN'T BE SEEN DEAD IN!)

Music

PLAY AWFUL, EASY-LISTENING
JAZZ MUSIC IN THE BACKGROUND.

AAGH! It's turning me off!
Stop it !!

Accesories

HAVE A SELECTION OF SEXY TOYS TO HAND.

A Playstation 2 ?!! That's not a sexy toy!

It is to me

Script

USE THE FOLLOWING SAMPLE SCRIPT AS A GUIDE:

```
Scene One - Front Door - Day

<DOORBELL RINGS>

HER:  Oh, HELLO there, handsome!!
      I'm all alone, you know!

HIM:  Hello Madam.  I'm here to
      fiddle with your pipes.

HER:  Ooooh yes, big boy!  They're
      dripping wet.  I think you need
      to stuff something up them.

HIM:  Don't worry, I'll give them a
      good going over.  Why don't I
      pull out my big tool and
      get to work.

HER:  OOOOOOOOOhhhh!  Tee hee hee!!!

<BONKING BEGINS>
```

MAUDE LEARNS NEVER
TO WEAR HIGH HEELS
IN A WATER BED

TO HER EMBARRASSMENT, MAUDE DISCOVERED SHE HAD V.P.L. (VISIBLE POO LINE)

Fun Games to play with a Willy!

1. Shadow Games!

2. Impressions of famous people!

3. Fish Bait!

4. The 'Find the Sausage in the Popcorn' game!

OTHER **ODD SQUAD** TITLES AVAILABLE:

TITLE	ISBN	PRICE
NEW! The Odd Squad's BIG POO HANDBOOK	1 84161 168 9	£7.99
The Odd Squad Little Book of... series		
BOOZE	1 84161 138 7	£2.50
OLDIES	1 84161 139 5	£2.50
MEN	1 84161 093 3	£2.50
POO	1 84161 096 8	£2.50
PUMPING	1 84161 140 9	£2.50
SEX	1 84161 095 X	£2.50
WOMEN	1 84161 094 1	£2.50
X-RATED CARTOONS	1 84161 141 7	£2.50
The Odd Squad Vol 1	1 85304 936 0	£3.99
The REAL Kama Sutra	1 84161 103 4	£3.99

Ordering...

Please send a cheque/postal order in £ sterling, made payable to 'Ravette Publishing Ltd' for the cover price of the book/s and allow the following for postage and packing...

UK & BFPO	50p for the first book & 30p per book thereafter
Europe & Eire	£1.00 for the first book & 50p per book thereafter
Rest of the world	£1.80 for the first book & 80p per book thereafter

RAVETTE PUBLISHING LTD
Unit 3, Tristar Centre
Star Road
Partridge Green
West Sussex RH13 8RA